The Feelings we've Forgotten

Eliana Tuley

The Feelings we've Forgotten © 2023 Eliana
Tuley

All rights reserved.

Eliana Tuley asserts the moral right to be
identified as author of this work.

Presentation by *BookLeaf Publishing*

Web: www.bookleafpub.com

E-mail: info@bookleafpub.com

ISBN: 9789357442534

First edition 2023

*To my amazing friends, family and everyone
who inspired my poems*

ACKNOWLEDGEMENT

#TheWriteAngle writing challenge

Shore of Shadows

The sun isn't awake and I'm alone,
Waiting here under the darkened sky
And right now the silence seems to groan
And I don't have the strength to wonder why.

I'm standing by the shore, a pool of tears.
Memories reflected on the sea,
All of the mistakes of all the years.
I see the monsters staring back at me.

Not strong enough to run away again
I just lie there tired on the ground,
While my blood is used to fuel this pen.
I'm feeling like I'm lost but won't be found.

I hate the way the world looks through a tear.
Hiding from the mirrors that I see.
Waiting for the beacon to appear
To show me what I am supposed to be.

And I just want to hear a friendly voice,
Something that I know in the commotion.
I don't feel like I have got a choice,
That doesn't end with drowning in this ocean.

Young Love

She's always on your mind you're losing sleep,
And honestly I've known that feeling too.
You told her how you feel you took the leap,
I know how hard a thing that is to do.
It hurts when someone doesn't like you back,
I've grown to know the feeling rather well.
You think of all the attributes you lack,
But you are worth much more than you can tell.
I know the ache of unrequited love,
How much it hurts how bad it makes you feel.
I know it's really nothing like we dreamed of,
And it will take some time for you to heal.
But if you feel alone it isn't true,
Because I feel the same way but for you.

The Sun's Goodnight

The golden light reflecting,
Off of every hope and dream.
The shadows, now respecting,
Every concentrated beam.

In a moment warm and bright,
A calm perfection settles.
Hope and peace lie in the light,
Like scattered flower petals.

Golden hour melts away,
Along with sunset skies,
But the soft light seems to say:
'I'll see you when I rise'.

Love Yourself

Running from the mirrors all around you,
You're hiding in the shadows all alone.
Try to cover up the things you've been through,
But also kind of wishing that they'd known.

For so long you've hated your reflection,
And now you're scared to show them who you
are.
Stumble on not knowing the direction,
Using all your wishes on a star.

And you might not see your inner beauty,
Or how strong you are underneath the scars.
Being their perfection's not your duty,
Cause truly you're the one among the stars.

So don't let the worthless words define you,
Cause you're above that even when it's hard.
And pretty stars of glass can shatter too,
But light reflects off every little shard.

Broken

I used to thank all of my stars,
That I wasn't where I am now
Abandoned behind prison bars
I'm hurt and I'm wondering how.

I'd never wish I was older,
Or wish I could change everything.
Promises keep feeling colder,
I'm scared what tomorrow will bring.

Feels like I'll never stop hurting,
Anxiety once was unknown.
Faking a smile's exerting,
And I've never felt more alone.

Butterflies

Floating by the empty sky,
But anxiously you're soaring.
When were happy you come by,
So things aren't ever boring.

Delicate as a young heart,
But just as fierce as fire.
Butterflies when we're apart,
And here for each desire.

Always watched with jealous eyes,
You're fluttering so free.
But my favorite butterflies,
Are the ones you give to me.

Look Ahead

Who do you want to be?
What will you do?
Where do you dream to see?
You must have thought it through.

What they expect of me,
I want to know.
I have no guarantee
Of where my life will go.

"The question is simple"
I disagree.
Each choice makes a ripple
That can come back to me.

My future is scary,
Leaves me confused.
The future will vary,
And it can leave us bruised.

Empty

Empty cloudless skies,
Freezing windblown hair.
Emotionless eyes,
No warmth left to spare.

Broken, deserted,
Forgotten, alone.
Whole life averted
From their hearts of stone.

Tired of waiting
For people to change.
Life is frustrating,
Society's strange.

Scared of the future
That used to be just,
Forgotten ruler,
In God they would trust.

The wars leave a scar,
And it's all a show.
Never know how far,
A smile can go.

To: L

Curly blonde hair that must shine in the sun,
With a smile that could melt any heart.
And our single dance was so much more fun,
Then all the rest of the dance from the start.

Friendly and charming and sweet the whole
time,
Felt like you were one of my oldest friends.
Been on my mind so I wrote you this rhyme,
Because I'm set now on making amends.

I didn't thank you but still you should know,
Just how grateful I was for that dance.
Hand that reached out to me when I was low,
And it started with a friendly glance.

Reflection

As long as you remember
It has been there every day.
Seen every tear and ember
And watched every smile fade.

Now almost invisible,
It's old and worn in our eyes.
Makes so many miserable,
Cause it doesn't show inside.

All hated our reflection
Once, cause it takes work to love.
Don't give it much affection,
Cause it's nothing new to us.

It is always sad to me,
That so often we complain
Then one day you look and see
And wonder when so much has changed.

Sceneries Left on My Heart

I'm looking at Sunset Skies,
I'm drowning in City Lights,
I'm wishing on Falling leaves,
I'm hoping for Starry nights.

Enjoying those Ocean views,
And strolling down Snowy lanes,
And walking the Sandy Beach ,
And dancing In Nighttime rain.

In love with the Mirror lakes,
In love with Those Misty eyes,
In love with the Fluffy clouds,
In love with that Pink Sunrise.

Enjoying those Stormy days,
Along with those Icy streets,
And also the Fresh green hill,
Enjoying this quiet peace.

In My Dreams

Holding you in my arms,
See the world in your eyes,
Can't live without your charms,
Got me on endless highs.

Love the way your voice sounds,
A way to lead me home.
Next to you sadness drowns.
Gentle as ocean foam.

Your love's as fierce as fire,
And still as soft as snow.
My only desire,
Never want to let go.

Here for You

Reach out to my hand,
We see you falling
And I understand
How it feels when dropping.

You've been here so long,
Fighting your way through,
I'll hold on, be strong
So that you don't have to.

I wish you could know,
We see your smiles.
And when the winds blow,
You're strong through the trials.

Smiles so selfless,
Your laugh I adore.
When I feel helpless,
You teach me to soar.

Last Night

Remember last night when you said you loved
me,
While we were dancing right under the stars,
You looked at me like I was all you could see.
We knew that someday the world would be ours.

I'd never felt safer than there in your arms,
It all felt like it was too good to stay.
Still I couldn't help but to soak in your charms,
I tried to hold on but it faded away.

Awoke in a land that was so far from you,
When my reality came to exist.
The cursed sun was shining, the irksome sky,
blue,
While your memory faded to mist.

Darkness

Wild, mysterious, dark secret fog,
That conceals every question unasked.
Try to ignore how we choke in the smog,
And pretend that our heroes aren't masked.

Creating the darkness we try to fight,
and distractions that mess with our mind.
Try to hold on to the last rays of light,
But so many still follow the blind.

My Best Friend

My best friend is always kind,
To anyone or thing.
My best friend is seldom shy,
But her words never sting.

My best friend is thoughtful first,
And then she speaks her mind.
My best friend is always there,
If my path I can't find.

My best friend inspires me,
To be a better girl.
And ever since she left us,
Her absence changed my world.

Crush

Escape from life when I think of your name,
But now you're slipping I don't know the way,
And I'll get hurt if you don't feel the same,
But pain is better than numb empty grey.
You're in my head no matter what they say,
Can't get you off my mind I've tried it all,
If only you could choose whether to fall.

Scared

Was my best friend and more than that
somehow,
But now I'm scared that you don't know my
name.
And I feel like I need you here right now,
But also really doubt you feel the same,

And you know I really want to see you,
But I'm scared of how different things could be.
Scared we've grown apart too much to undo.
I'm scared that you won't like the me you see.

Scared we changed and we won't know who we
were,
Scared you moved on and forgot I exist.
Scared that you're happier alone with her,
Scared my memory has faded to mist.

Scared our friendship won't ever be the same.
Scared I didn't mean more to you than we knew.
Scared you will think the way I feel is lame.
Scared that this will never matter to you.

18

My Boy

Long ago you said that my eyes sparkled,
Like a river underneath the Moon.
You meant so much to me, wish you knew it,
I'm scared to death but hope to see you soon.

Once upon a time you said my lips were,
In your own words, as soft as a rose.
We were young but so happy, I miss that.
I wish I knew where the precious time goes.

And then one day you told me my skin was,
Just as smooth as still waters could be.
Taught me young how a good guy should treat
us.
I miss how great a friend you were to me.

Anna

All the girls wish they were like you,
Nice to all, confident and strong.
Never try to make anyone feel bad,
And the friend that was there all along.

Life

Life brings us hurt and pains,
Healing takes time.
People leave scars and stains
On the inside.

Our feelings are played with,
We put up walls.
Is everything a myth?
Confidence falls.

Loved ones can betray you,
Is trust alive?
This world leaves us broken,
Out and inside.

And so simple kindness,
Goes really far,
And helps to remind us,
Just how needed we are.

Printed in the USA
CPSIA information can be obtained
at www.ICGtesting.com
LVHW011541050124
767941LV00091B/5164